National Defense Research Ins

ENLISTED PERSONNEL TRENDS

IN THE SELECTED RESERVE, 1986–1994

An Executive Summary

SHEILA NATARAJ KIRBY

RICHARD BUDDIN

Prepared for the Office of the Secretary of Defense

RAND

This report is an executive summary of a study examining personnel readiness of the Selected Reserve Components from FY86–FY94. The study results are reported in a companion document, MR-681/2-OSD, which describes the data, technical analyses, and findings in detail and will serve as a reference source for future work in this area. This summary sets the overall findings in a policy context and highlights their importance. In addition, it points to some potential areas of concern with respect to reserve manning in the future. The study builds on earlier work on reserve personnel readiness that was based on the FY89 inventory of reserve personnel and was reported in Grissmer et al. (1994a). That report highlighted a potential constraint to relying on the reserve force: the likelihood of future limits on the availability of experienced formerly active-duty personnel for reserve service resulting from the active drawdown.

The current study updates and extends the earlier analysis in a number of important ways. First, the data examined are more recent (through FY94) and reflect the early effects of both the active and the reserve drawdown; second, analyses of the large cohorts recently separated from active duty point to the success of the Reserve Components in recruiting from this prior-service pool; third, fears that Operation Desert Storm might lead to a huge outflow from the reserves can largely be laid to rest, as the analysis of attrition shows. Indeed, the study reveals that the Reserve Components have been remarkably successful in keeping quality high, attracting and retaining prior-service personnel, improving skill match rates at entry, and keeping attrition and skill-qualification rates fairly stable.

This work was sponsored by the Assistant Secretary for Reserve Affairs. The research was conducted in the Forces and Resources Policy Center, which is part of RAND's National Defense Research Institute, a federally funded research and development center sponsored by the Office of the Secretary of Defense, the Joint Staff, and the defense agencies.

CONTENTS

FIGURES

We wish to thank Frank Rush and Wayne Spruell for their support of this study and the Defense Manpower Data Center for providing the data that form the basis of the analysis. Dan Kohner of Reserve Affairs was helpful in providing data on current and planned end-strengths. The report benefited greatly from the helpful comments provided by our RAND colleagues, Ron Sortor and Harry Thie, who reviewed a draft of the final report, and Susan Hosek. We thank David Grissmer for several useful discussions during the course of the analysis and Jerry Sollinger for his suggestions on how to improve the readability and clarity of the report. We are grateful to Patricia Bedrosian for her careful and patient editing.

AFR	Air Force Reserve
ANG	Air National Guard
AT	Annual Training
DoD	Department of Defense
ETS	Enlisted Term of Service
HSG	High School Graduate
IADT	Initial Active Duty Training
MCR	Marine Corps Reserve
NCO	Noncommissioned Officer
NPS	Nonprior Service
NR	Naval Reserve
NTC	National Training Center
ODS/S	Operation Desert Shield/Storm
OSD	Office of the Secretary of Defense
PS	Prior service
RCCPD	Reserve Component Common Personnel Data System
TAFMS	Total Active Federal Military Service
USAR	U.S. Army Reserve

ENLISTED PERSONNEL TRENDS IN THE SELECTED RESERVE, 1986–1994: AN EXECUTIVE SUMMARY

BACKGROUND

The American military is undergoing a fundamental reshaping and restructuring brought about by the changing political and military global environment, changing domestic priorities, and tighter fiscal constraints. The "Total Force" Policy instituted in 1973 clearly specified that reserve forces would be "the initial and primary augmentation of active forces and military response would involve the integrated use of all forces available including active, reserve, civilian, and allied" (Brauner, Thie, and Brown, 1992, p. 1). During the 1980s, the Reserve Components grew rapidly as they were given increasingly demanding missions. Before the beginning of the drawdown, the Selected Reserve forces were the largest and most experienced in recent history. Reserve Component endstrength peaked in FY89 at nearly 1.2 million Selected Reserve members. Operation Desert Storm provided an important reminder of the greater reliance on reserve forces. Over 245,000 reservists were mobilized. The October 1993 *Report on the Bottom-Up Review* by then Secretary of Defense Les Aspin recognized the Reserve Component forces as an integral part of our armed forces and "essential to the implementation of our defense strategy" (Aspin, 1993, p. 91).

Since then, as Figure 1 shows, reserve forces have been drawing down, although not to the extent that the active forces have. Reserve endstrength has declined by 14.7 percent from FY89 to FY94, and it is planned that the reserve will stabilize at just under 900,000 by the end of the drawdown. This will represent a 25 percent reduction from peak strength in FY89. The reserve drawdown is thus two-thirds complete.

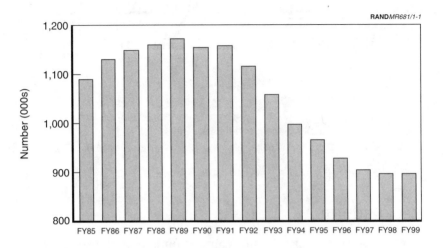

Figure 1—Selected Reserve Endstrengths, FY85–FY99

Despite the drawdown, fiscal constraints are placing a high priority on using reserve forces wherever they can meet deployment dates and readiness criteria. Currently, for example, the Air National Guard (ANG) provides all of the nation's air defense; the U.S. Army Reserve (USAR) provides all the chemical brigades and heavy helicopter units and about 70 percent of the medical assets of the Army; the Air Force Reserve (AFR) provides half the air crews for troop and supply movement to combat areas; 90 percent of cargo handling and shipping control is in the purview of the Naval Reserve (NR); and the Marine Corps Reserve (MCR) provides one of the four Marine divisions. It is expected that, by FY99, the Reserve Components will constitute 39 percent of the nation's defense force—up from 36 percent at the end of the Cold War.

In addition, the Reserve Components are expected to play an important role in responding to regional crises, as well as in peacekeeping, peace enforcement, and humanitarian assistance operations. Indeed, Reserve Component involvement in peacekeeping and humanitarian assistance operations, although still fairly limited, increased significantly over the past few years, as evidenced by the Army MFO Sinai Initiative, reserve support of Somalia's Operations RESTORE HOPE and PROVIDE RELIEF, the 1993 Kiev medical mission, and numerous others (Aspin, 1993, pp. 41–54). Reservists have been an important part of the Bosnian and Somalian support sorties as well as the domestic emergency teams responding to floods, earthquakes, and hurricane-hit areas. The Assistant Secretary of Defense for Reserve Affairs, Deborah Lee, explicated the current strategy: "As we reduce the size of the Active component, we must use the National Guard and Reserve as a form of compensating leverage to reduce risks and contain defense costs in the post–Cold War era" (Department of Defense, 1994).

THE FOCUS OF THIS REPORT

These roles and missions, combined with the downsizing of the active forces, make the personnel sustentation of the reserve—that is, the ability of the reserve to meet the manpower and readiness requirements called for by our national military strategy—a critical issue. To a large extent, "the sustentation of the reserve depends crucially on the ability of the reserve to accomplish three objectives: recruit and retain prior-service (PS) personnel from the active forces; utilize their prior training effectively; and maintain low levels of attrition for all reserve personnel" (Grissmer and Kirby, 1994, p. 190).

This report focuses on the Selected Reserve enlisted force and its changing profile, set against the context of the military drawdown and the end of the Cold War. The main emphasis is on changes from FY89 through FY94. The report addresses four issues:

- Attracting and retaining prior-service personnel from the active forces;

- Effectively using their prior training;

- Maintaining low levels of attrition for all reserve personnel; and,

- Maintaining high levels of skill qualification in units.

It tracks the recent performance of the Selected Reserve Components on these fronts against the policy context of Operation Desert Storm and the downsizing of both the active and the reserve forces.

The drawdown of the active forces raises some serious concerns regarding the ability of the reserves to meet PS content goals and maintain the required levels of readiness, as discussed in our earlier report

(Grissmer et al., 1994a). The active force provides experienced personnel to the reserve forces; as the size of the active force declines, so would the flow of personnel with active-duty experience to the reserve forces. If these prior-service personnel are critical to the readiness of the Reserve Components and the size of the reserve components remains stable, reserve readiness would also decline.

Along with this potential disruption in the pipeline of prior-service personnel from the Active Component to the Reserve Component, especially for components that are already supply-constrained such as the Army Reserve Components, the report mentioned several other personnel problems facing the Reserve Components. These included high attrition and turnover among personnel—both those with and those without prior active service—and the large number of individuals in reserve units who are not skill-qualified. In FY89, this level was between 20 and 30 percent for the Army components.

The earlier report (Grissmer et al., 1994a) provided a snapshot of the Reserve Components at the end of FY89 in terms of the mix of prior active service and nonprior-service personnel, linked PS content to various personnel readiness issues, projected how the PS content would change for each component under alternative active and reserve force sizes and mixes, and estimated a potential reduction in PS content (particularly for the Army components).

Some dramatic changes have recently occurred on the military front, and these have changed the environment in which the reserves operate in significant ways. We elaborate on these changes below.

POLICY CONTEXT

Four major factors set the context for the study and need to be accounted for in our analysis:

- The potential fallout from participation in Operation Desert Storm;
- Congressional concern about the readiness of reserve units called up for Operation Desert Storm;
- The drawdown of active forces; and
- The drawdown of reserve forces.

First, Operation Desert Shield/Storm provided the first major test of Total Force Policy. It represented the first large-scale call-up and use of the reserve forces since the Korean War; the first major conflict under the Department of Defense's (DoD) Total Force Policy; and the first call-up using the new authority to access reserves provided by the Congress in 1976 (Brauner, Thie, and Brown, 1992, p. xiii).

There were fears that the actual use of reserves would cause potential major problems in recruiting and retention. This fear stemmed partly from earlier evidence regarding the effect of extended training on retention. Studies of Army National Guard units selected for National Training Center (NTC) participation for their annual training (AT) during the 1983–1985 time period showed significantly higher attrition among these units, relative to comparable units that were not selected to participate in this initiative. The NTC training increased the time required for AT (three weeks instead of the usual two weeks) and also required that units undertake a more intense training schedule in the year preceding NTC—the so-called NTC train-up, usually in the form of several extra days of drills over the year. Results showed that there was a 29 percent increase in unit attrition and a 25 percent increase in Guard attrition potentially attributable to NTC training (Grissmer and Nogami, 1988), and survey data revealed that reservists faced increased family conflicts and employer problems because of the new training schedule.

Further evidence on the likely effects of extended training time comes from the 1986 Reserve Components Survey. Those results showed that extra drills or longer AT would reduce reenlistment rates of both junior and senior enlisted personnel by 7 to 13 percent (Grissmer, Buddin, and Kirby, 1989). In addition, Grissmer, Kirby, and Sze (1992) found that perceived family and employer attitudes tended to be the most important predictors of reenlistment among those making early to mid-career decisions (those with 4–12 years of service). Given the preponderance of this earlier evidence and the anecdotal data from reservists called up during the six-month ODS/S mobilization regarding economic losses, loss in employer-provided benefits, and family hardships, the mobilization caused grave concern among military manpower planners regarding the potential effect of the mobilization on current and future recruiting and retention.

Second, Congressional concern about the lack of readiness of some units of the ARNG during ODS/S led to the passage of Title XI—the Army National Guard Combat Readiness Reform Act (U.S. House of Representatives, 1993, p. 231). The legislation set PS content goals for the ARNG of 50 percent of enlisted members and 65 percent of officers; these goals were to be met by FY97. The definition of prior active service was two years of active-duty experience. For the first time, the Guard was faced with legislated goals for types of personnel in an environment that, as we pointed out above, could make meeting these goals more difficult in the future.

Third, the active drawdown, which began in 1990, has substantially decreased the size of the active forces. Operation Desert Shield/ Storm delayed the planned active force drawdown, and the DoD stoploss policy during the Gulf War reduced active-duty separations to nearly zero in late 1990 and early 1991. As a result, the active force had relatively few losses in FY91 and an extraordinary number of losses in FY92. Figure 2 shows that the active force drawdown has been the most severe in the Army where enlisted endstrength has declined by 31 percent since FY89. The force reduction in the Air Force is the next largest at 26 percent. The size of the Navy declined by 22 percent and the Marine Corps had the smallest decline in endstrength: 12 percent between FY89 and FY94.

In addition, further cuts are planned through FY99. Army enlisted endstrength will stabilize at about 411,000 by FY96—a decline of 9 percent from FY94 levels. Present plans call for a decline in Navy enlisted endstrength of 16.5 percent from the FY94 levels to 336,000. The Marine Corps endstrength will fall by a negligible 300 to 156,000 and the Air Force faces a further 11 percent reduction to an endstrength of 303,000 by FY99.

Fourth, the Selected Reserve drawdown has differentially affected different Reserve Components. Reserve enlisted endstrength peaked in 1989 and has declined by about 15 percent since then. This pattern varies somewhat across components. The decline has been most dramatic in the Naval Reserve where strength levels have declined by 30 percent relative to their 1989 levels. The reserve drawdown has also had large effects on the two Army components with the Army National Guard and Army Reserve declining by 14 and 20

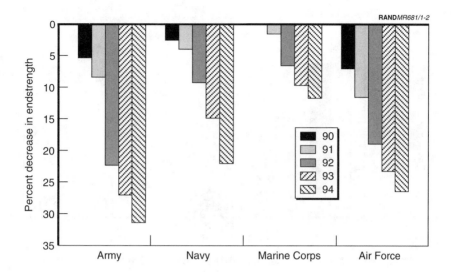

RAND_MR681/1-2_

Figure 2—Percentage Decrease in Active-Duty Enlisted
Endstrength Relative to FY89

percent, respectively. The Marine Corps Reserve and Air components had much smaller reductions in strength.

The reserve drawdown means that the demand for new personnel
was weaker in the past few years than during the period from FY86
through FY89 when reserve endstrength was relatively stable or increasing. All components are shrinking somewhat, but the declines
are most pronounced in the NR and USAR. On the other hand, the
supply of prior-service personnel available to the Selected Reserve
has been unusually large in the past few years.

As with the active force, further reductions in Selected Reserve endstrength of about 11 percent are planned. As Figure 3 shows, the
components will be differentially affected by the planned cuts, with
the USAR being hit the hardest. ARNG endstrength will decline by 8
percent from FY94 to FY99 to 323,349, and the USAR endstrength will
be cut by about 19 percent from approximately 207,000 in FY94 to
168,000 by FY99. The NR faces a decline in endstrength of about 12
percent, whereas the Air Reserve Components face somewhat

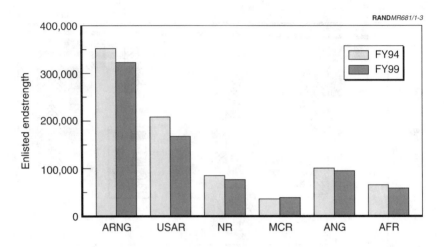

**Figure 3—Selected Reserve Enlisted Endstrength by Component,
FY94 and FY99**

smaller cuts: 7 percent (ANG) and 9 percent (AFR). No cuts are planned for the Marine Corps Reserve.

In such a changing and uncertain environment, it is important to assess what progress the reserve forces have made in the recent time period in achieving the four objectives listed above. This can also provide a benchmark for military manpower planners dealing with future manning issues. The analyses reported here help fill this gap. Along with the detailed analyses provided in MR-681/2-OSD, the companion report, they provide a comprehensive look at the Reserve Components along a variety of readiness dimensions.

DATA

Our data comprise two sets of personnel files:

1. For each reservist from FY85 through FY94, we use quarterly snapshots taken from the Reserve Components Common Personnel Data System (RCCPDS) master files. These were matched by Social Security Number to provide a longitudinal history of each reservist.

2. For the accession analysis, we use active loss files from FY86 through FY94 matched to the reserve master files to see if and when individuals leaving the active force join the Selected Reserve.

These more recent data allow us to examine how successful the Selected Reserve Components have been in meeting the four objectives outlined earlier as being crucial to reserve personnel readiness and manning.

MR-681/2-OSD provides substantial further detail on these and other related questions.

Before we address the four specific issues addressed by our analysis, a brief profile of the Selected Reserve Components is provided to set the context for the subsequent discussions.

PROFILE OF SELECTED RESERVE COMPONENTS

The components differ markedly in their dependence on prior-service personnel, ranging from 70 percent in the Air Force Reserve to 35 percent in the two Army components (see Figure 4).[1] However,

---

[1]The Congressional goals defined prior service as 24 months of active duty. Presumably this was set to correspond to the shortest active-duty term available to enlistees. However, as we discussed in our earlier report (Grissmer et al., 1994a), the Congressional language failed to specify precisely what constituted "active duty." Reservists are given credit for active duty when attending two weeks of annual training, initial active duty for training (IADT), or when attending certain military schools for training. By attending IADT, annual training over a number of years, and other associated training schools, a reservist with no prior active service could accumulate sufficient active-duty days over a period of years to meet the Congressional definition. Presumably the intent of Congress was not to include such individuals in the PS definition. Therefore, our definition attempts to count only continuous active service as a member of the active component by excluding annual training days.

More precisely, we estimate the months of active duty by adjusting the data field—total active federal military service (TAFMS)—obtained from the Reserve Components Common Personnel Data System records that form our main source of data. TAFMS measures months of active-duty military service but also includes time spent in annual training, IADT, and other formal school training in active-duty schools. Although we do not have the data that would allow us to fully adjust TAFMS, we do adjust for the increment due to annual training days. This is done by subtracting annual training days that accrue to TAFMS throughout the reserve career. Our earlier analysis of FY88–FY89 data showed that the ARNG and MCR did not increment TAFMS

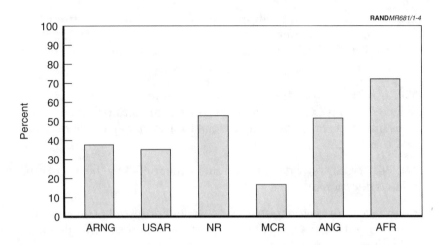

Figure 4—Percentage of Nonprior-Service Personnel in Part-Time Enlisted Inventory, FY94

the numbers for ARNG (PS content of 43 percent even factoring in full-time personnel) point to the difficulty of meeting Title XI goals, which were set at 50 percent PS content for the enlisted force and 65 percent for the officer force. As the active force continues to draw down, it may become harder to maintain or increase these PS levels in the future.

The current reserve force is very senior and very experienced in terms of years of service, as shown in Figure 5. The proportion of nonprior-service (NPS) individuals (i.e., those without any prior military experience) in the inventory has declined from 18 percent in FY89 to 13 percent in FY94. Over 40 percent of the FY94 part-time enlisted personnel have 10 or more years of service; about 25 percent have 15 or more years of service.

In addition, the active-duty experience level has risen. In FY89, close to 60 percent of PS personnel had between 2 and 4 years of active-duty service. By FY94, this group accounts for only 45 percent of all

---

for annual training days. For these components, we used TAFMS directly rather than the adjusted TAFMS. Using this corrected TAFMS measure, we defined as PS those with TAFMS≥ 24 months.

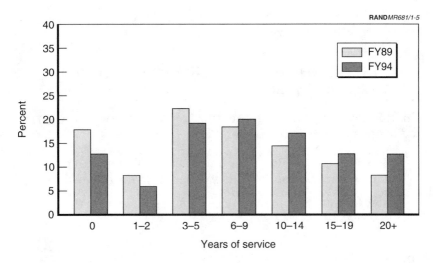

Figure 5—Percentage of Part-Time Enlisted Personnel by Years of Service,
FY89 and FY94

PS personnel, and there is a concomitant rise in the proportion of PS
personnel with more than 4 years of service.

Table 1 summarizes the changes in the inventory profile over time.

Table 1

Summary of Changes in Inventory Profile, FY89–FY94

Selected Reserve Component	Inventory PS Content	Inventory Active Experience	Inventory Quality (HSG/Cat I–IIIA)[a]
ARNG	Higher	Greater	Higher/higher
USAR	Higher	Greater	Higher/higher
NR	Higher	Greater	Higher/stable
MCR	Higher	Greater	Higher/higher
ANG	Higher	Greater	Higher/higher
AFR	Higher	Greater	Higher/stable

[a]Recruits are classified into percentile groups labeled Category I, Category II,
Category IIIA, Category IIIB, Category IV, and Category V mental groups, based
on scores received on the entrance examination (Armed Forces Qualification
Test, or AFQT). Cat I–IIIA are those scoring at or above the 50th percentile.

We turn now to an examination of the recent progress made in attaining specific objectives.

RECRUITING AND RETAINING NEW PRIOR ACTIVE SERVICE PERSONNEL

In this section, we examine the trends in new prior-service affiliations with the Selected Reserve:

- How well are the Reserve Components doing in attracting new prior-service personnel as they depart from the active force?

- How long are new prior-service personnel staying in the Selected Reserve?

Recruiting

An important leading indicator of Selected Reserve problems is the reserves' success—or lack thereof—in attracting new prior-service personnel from the pool separating from the active force. These prior-service personnel enhance reserve readiness by enriching the experience base of the force and saving training resources. These savings are particularly large if the recruit is assigned a reserve position in his/her active-duty skill, since this job match maximizes the return on his/her experience and obviates the delay and cost associated with retraining.

After the drawdown, the Selected Reserve will face a potential crisis in personnel supply if the flow of new prior-service personnel is substantially reduced. In the short term, however, the active drawdown increased the number of separatees available to the reserve. It was unclear whether the reserve could capitalize on the drawdown to enhance their prior-service content with losses from the active-duty force. Similarly, we were uncertain whether active-duty personnel affected by the drawdown would be less enthusiastic about affiliating with a Selected Reserve unit than those in the earlier Cold War era had been. The changing roles, missions, and perceptions of the military and the Selected Reserve might also have changed the predisposition of departing active-duty personnel to affiliate with a reserve unit. In particular, the Selected Reserve deployment in ODS/S might have changed attitudes toward affiliation with a local reserve unit.

In this section, we focus on individuals who were released from active service at the expiration of their term of service (ETS) or who were released as part of an early release program. These individuals constitute the prime prior active service market available to the Selected Reserve Components. Other active-duty separatees are attrition losses, and their separation conditions frequently limit their eligibility for joining the Selected Reserve. In some cases, special waivers allow individuals discharged from the active force for medical or behavioral problems to affiliate with the reserve. Nevertheless, the vast majority of new affiliates come from the group of individuals who satisfactorily complete their active-duty terms (Buddin and Kirin, 1994; Marquis and Kirby, 1989).

The analysis examines two groups of active-duty losses: junior personnel with 2–6 years of active-duty experience and mid-career personnel with 7–12 years of active-duty experience.[2] These two groups constitute individuals who have served one term in the active force (or possibly have reenlisted once or have extended their initial enlistment) and those who are separating from the career force. We treat the two groups separately, because we anticipated that they might have different interest in joining the Selected Reserve, and the reserve might have different demands for personnel with different experience levels.

We examine both affiliation rates and number of affiliations to address the first issue raised above. However, the total number of affiliations results from the interaction of supply and demand arising from unit vacancies in the Reserve Components and does not merely reflect the propensities of prior-service personnel to enlist in the reserves. As a result, one needs to be cautious when drawing inferences from these trends, particularly during periods of drawdown.

---

[2] There are very few losses among individuals with more than 12 years of service.

Affiliations

Army. Among junior personnel, the overall affiliation rate has been stable over the eight years examined, but the composition of reserve gains has shifted from the USAR to the ARNG. In FY93, the total affiliation rate for junior personnel was somewhat higher than in FY86 (44 versus 41 percent), but the composition had shifted dramatically: The ARNG attracted 26 percent of separatees compared with 18 percent for the USAR. We can speculate as to the reasons: ARNG had more vacancies or had a policy of overmanning, individuals preferred ARNG to USAR because of inherent differences between the two components, or preferential treatment was given to PS individuals by the Guard.

The affiliation patterns for mid-career personnel are similar, but the overall affiliation rate among mid-career personnel has been somewhat lower in most years.

The stability of the overall affiliation rate means that the Army Reserve components have succeeded in capturing unusually large numbers of prior-service personnel from the drawdown, and this was partly reflected in the higher PS content of the components reported earlier. In the case of mid-career personnel, the ARNG and USAR absorbed nearly three times as many new prior-service gains from the FY92 cohort as from previous Army loss cohorts. Junior losses in FY92 were also considerably larger than those of the FY88 through FY90 cohorts, so the number of junior-level affiliations increased by about 20 percent.

Navy. The affiliation rate of both junior and mid-career Navy separatees has fallen off somewhat from the rates of the late 1980s. The declining rates are applied to a larger base number of losses in the recent cohorts, however, so the total number of affiliations with the NR has increased slightly among junior personnel and declined by about 10 percent for mid-career personnel. Declining NR affiliation rates might well reflect the limited availability of positions in the NR. The NR is reducing its endstrength substantially, as shown earlier in Figure 2, so Navy losses might have difficulties finding NR positions to fill.

Marine Corps. The MCR has traditionally had a very low level of prior-service content as a matter of policy. The enlisted ranks of the MCR are drawn predominantly from nonprior-service personnel, and affiliations from the MCR to the USMC are more common than the reverse. The limited MCR demand for prior-service personnel is an important factor in the decision of many Marine Corps personnel to affiliate with other Selected Reserve Components (primarily the ARNG and less often the USAR).

The overall probability of affiliating with the Selected Reserve is smaller for Marine Corps personnel than for those from any other service branch. In FY93, the affiliation rates for junior personnel from the Army, Navy, and Air Force were 44, 16, and 33 percent, respectively, compared with only 11 percent for junior-level Marines. This low affiliation rate may well reflect the fact that in-service USMC recruiters have few MCR positions to fill. Nonetheless, the pool of USMC personnel is a potential resource for ARNG and USAR units that need prior-service personnel in related job skills.

The MCR affiliation rate has declined somewhat over recent cohorts, whereas the small flow of USMC personnel to other Selected Reserve Components has been relatively stable.

Air Force. The Active Air Force drawdown actually began in FY86. These reductions involved management actions to allow special early release programs in FY88 and FY90. FY92 also saw large losses of mid-career Air Force personnel as part of a broader OSD-level attempt to reduce endstrength.

The overall affiliation rate of Air Force personnel has varied somewhat over time, but the trend is slightly downward. The affiliation rate for junior personnel fell from 26 percent in FY86 to 23 percent in FY93; the downward trend is evident among mid-career personnel as well. The affiliation rate has been very responsive to the size of the respective loss cohorts. This relationship between affiliations and losses reflects the fact that the Air components are well staffed with prior-service personnel and have low attrition rates (Grissmer et al., 1994a), so the Air components have fewer positions to fill than other components.

First-Year Reserve Attrition of New Prior-Service Gains

How long do newcomers remain in the Selected Reserve? Gains in reserve affiliation would provide little long-term benefit if those gains were offset by higher reserve attrition.

The ARNG attrition rate has fallen substantially for both junior and mid-career personnel. Junior-level attrition has fallen from 25 percent in FY86 to 14 percent in FY93. Among new mid-career members, first-year attrition has been somewhat erratic but the post-ODS/S attrition rates for mid-career personnel have been 8 to 10 percentage points lower than for the earlier years.

For the USAR, first-year attrition rates for new prior-service gains were quite high in FY86, but the rates have fallen substantially since then. In FY86, the attrition rates for new junior and mid-career personnel were 46 and 35 percent, respectively. These have declined to 27 and 33 percent for junior and mid-career personnel, respectively, in FY93, but are still quite high.

Like the USAR, NR first-year attrition rates are quite large. In FY86, these rates for junior and mid-career prior-service gains were 50 and 37 percent, respectively. The attrition rates in the FY93 cohort have declined to 37 and 31 percent for junior and mid-career personnel. These large loss rates mean that the NR (like the USAR) is not receiving much benefit from many of its prior-service gains.

The MCR does not use many prior-service personnel, but the evidence shows that the MCR attrition rates for new prior-service personnel were extraordinarily high before the drawdown. Among junior personnel, the first-year loss rate declined from 62 percent in FY86 to 23 percent in FY93. Senior personnel attrition has also improved substantially since the end of the Cold War.

The ANG has historically had much lower first-year attrition than any of the other components, and the ANG has substantially reduced this loss rate since the end of the Cold War. Among junior personnel, the attrition rate has fallen from 17 percent in FY86 to only 6 percent in FY93. The separation rate for mid-career personnel has been erratic, but the trend has also been downward. Senior-level attrition was 16 percent in FY86 but leveled off at 9 percent by FY92.

The attrition marks for the AFR are better than those of the USAR, NR, and MCR, but the AFR has higher first-year attrition rates than either of the Guard components. As with the other components, first-year loss rates have declined substantially since the 1980s. Attrition rates among junior personnel have fallen from 37 percent in FY86 to 19 percent in FY93. The mid-career attrition rate has been rather stable, but it has fallen by 3 percentage points over the eight year period.

In summary, then, the Reserve Components are doing well in attracting prior-service personnel during the active force drawdown. Table 2 provides a benchmark summary of this section. The early signs show that the reserves are continuing to attract prior-service personnel in the post–Cold War era. Affiliation rates have declined in the USAR, NR, MCR, and AFR, but they are improving in the ARNG. These lower rates are applied to a larger base, however, so the numbers of prior-service affiliations have been higher in all but the AFR and ANG.

All components are doing a better job of retaining these new prior-service gains. Reserve attrition has declined, so the reserves are getting more service from recent prior-service gains than from those of the Cold War era.

Table 2

Summary of New Prior Service Gains

Selected Reserve Component	Affiliation Rate	Affiliation Numbers	Reserve Attrition
ARNG	Better	Better	Better
USAR	Worse	Better	Better
NR	Worse	Better	Better
MCR	Worse	Better	Better
ANG	Stable	Stable	Better
AFR	Worse	Stable	Better

USE OF PRIOR SKILLS: SKILL MATCH AT ENTRY

Selected Reserve units will enhance the value of prior-service personnel in their units by matching individual active-duty and reserve job assignments. Unmatched members will need retraining for their reserve positions. This retraining is costly and substantially delays the member in becoming fully proficient at his/her new job assignment (Buddin and Grissmer, 1994).

The job matching problem is largely unique to the reserve. In the active force, personnel are trained to fill unit openings and are then moved to the location where positions are available. Some shortfalls and overages will occur, but the training base trains personnel full-time and assigns them to different units, as needed. In contrast, a Selected Reserve unit must recruit personnel in its vicinity to fill openings in the unit. In some cases, prior-service personnel might not have the job skills required in the local unit, and only distant units might have positions available that match the soldier's active-duty job. Units must fill some vacancies by training the new member in the assigned job. Alternatively, the unit might forgo the mismatched prior-service soldier, recruit a nonprior-service member for the unit, and send the recruit to basic and initial skill training in the required job.

High job match rates may not be a panacea for the reserve, because they may reflect a very restricted management policy. All other things being equal, the reserve would always prefer to match new prior-service recruits with unit vacancies. Unfortunately, the prior-service supply of individuals with the appropriate job skills in that geographical area might be thin, so the unit vacancy might remain unfilled for some time if the unit insists on a job match. Similarly, the affiliation rate might be artificially depressed if interested prior-service personnel are discouraged from joining the unit because their job skills are not needed.

ARNG and USAR

In the junior ranks, the ARNG has made dramatic progress in improving its job match rate: The match rate improved from 42 percent in FY86 to 65 percent in FY93. The USAR match rate rose in the late 1980s, then fell in the early 1990s, and the FY93 level is nearly the same as that in FY86. These changes mean that the 30 percentage point advantage of the USAR in job match has narrowed to only 6 percentage points in FY93.

The ARNG and USAR might have improved their job match marks in FY92 when large losses were available to them for filling vacancies. This did not occur, but the components did sustain relatively high match rates (especially by historical standards in the ARNG) while absorbing a much larger number of junior personnel.

Among mid-career personnel, the USAR has been consistently better than the ARNG at matching new prior-service personnel with their active-duty jobs. The ARNG has improved its match rate over time and the rate has declined in the USAR, so the gap between the two components has narrowed from 20 percentage points in FY86 to 10 percentage points in FY93. The USAR match rate for mid-career personnel has varied considerably over these few years from 72 percent in FY88 to only 59 percent in FY90.

Mid-career personnel have a somewhat lower job match rate in both components than do junior personnel. This reflects the fact that the job matching problems increase with rank and experience, since a noncommissioned officer (NCO) will have more difficulties finding a suitable job match in a local unit.

NR and MCR

The match rates in the NR are much lower than in the other components, but the rates have been rising in recent cohorts. The NR match rate does not vary much between junior and mid-career personnel—the match rate for both groups was 35 percent in FY86 and had risen to 46 percent by FY93.

The match rates for junior personnel in the MCR have been more volatile than those of the mid-career personnel, but the overall trend has been toward improvement. For junior personnel, the match rate was 58 percent in FY86, and it improved to 63 percent in FY93. For mid-career personnel, the number of new affiliates is small, but the match rate improved from 54 percent in FY86 to 63 percent in FY93.

ANG and AFR

The Air Reserve Components have historically had high match rates. This rate reflects, in part, that they have traditionally had long queues of active-duty personnel wishing to enlist in the reserve, so the ANG and AFR may have some discretion in choosing members that have appropriate active-duty skills.

Junior-level match rates have improved for both the ANG and the AFR. The ANG rate rose from 54 percent in FY86 to 69 percent in FY93. The match rate in FY92 was unusually low for the ANG at 51 percent. The job match rate is slightly higher in the AFR than in the ANG, and the AFR match rate rose from 65 percent in FY86 to 70 percent in FY93.

Senior-level match rates have declined substantially for the ANG since FY86, but the rates for the AFR are unchanged. In the ANG, the job match rate declined from 68 percent in FY86 to 58 percent in FY93. Match rates in the AFR have been volatile, but the FY86 rate of 66 percent was equivalent to that in FY93. A possible explanation for the sharp changes in the match rate from FY87 through FY91 is the large swings in active Air Force losses due to early release programs. The AFR might have achieved higher match rates from the large loss cohorts in FY88 and FY90, because they could select from among a larger cohort of losses to fill unit vacancies. However, this fails to explain, why a corresponding "spike" did not occur in the AFR match rate in FY92, when the mid-career loss cohort was also large because of special drawdown programs.

Overall, then, the reserves have improved the use of prior-service personnel by improving the job match of new members. The job match rates have increased in all components but the USAR. The match rate in the USAR has been stable, but the USAR has sustained a relatively high match rate while absorbing large numbers of new prior-service gains during the active Army drawdown.

ATTRITION IN THE RESERVE COMPONENTS

Attrition of trained personnel from the reserve is costly both in terms of the high recruiting and training costs it imposes (in addition to the loss of training investment in the individual) and in terms of its detrimental effect on the readiness of units.

Inventory Attrition

Inventory attrition is the major determinant, along with end-strengths, of the demand for replacement reservists. It provides an aggregated rate of turnover from the reserves. Our main focus is on FY89–FY93 inventories.

Annual attrition for the inventory as a whole has remained remarkably stable—a little over 21 percent left the reserve in both FY89 and FY93, and there appears to be little difference in attrition of all types of personnel. Contrary to gloomy predictions, Operation Desert Storm does not appear to have spawned a huge outflow of reservists in the succeeding years. The slight rise in inventory attrition for the later-year inventories could be the result of the drawdown as units were reorganized or closed down.

Attrition rates for prior-service enlisted personnel by *active* years of service show surprisingly little difference in annual attrition rates, regardless of the level of active experience. On average, 20–22 percent of PS individuals leave the reserve every year, regardless of how senior they are or how much experience they brought with them into the reserve. It is interesting to note that the rates appear to have fallen slightly over time.

There are large differences in attrition rates across components, as shown in Figure 6. The lowest attrition rates are among the two Air components, where annual attrition is between 10 and 15 percent. The ARNG has an overall attrition rate of 21 percent, and this has fallen to 19 percent for the FY93 inventory. The USAR, NR, and MCR experience loss rates from inventory of between 22 and 30 percent.

The inventory loss rate has increased modestly in almost every component (and markedly in the NR) for FY93 reservists without prior active service experience.

Attrition Rates of Gain Cohorts

It is important to distinguish between attrition of gains and that of inventory because the former may be driven by very different factors

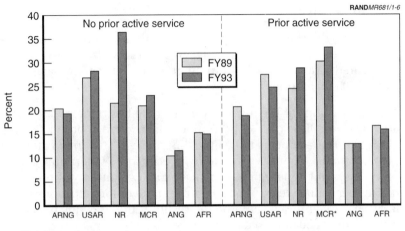

*Small sample size.

Figure 6—Annual Attrition Rates by Reserve Component and Type of Personnel, FY89 and FY93

and will probably be a better predictor of likely near-future attrition. New entrants to the reserve force are reacting to the immediate environment and reflecting the effects of recent policies, whereas the inventory may be dominated by individuals with strong ties to the reserve and strong ties to the retirement system.

We distinguish between NPS accessions, who enter without *any* prior military experience, and prior active service accessions.

Approximately 20 percent of NPS gains leave within one year of joining. The comparable attrition rate for prior-service gains, both reserve and active, is considerably higher—between 30 and 35 percent. However, one distinction that should be made is that early NPS attrition is unprogrammed attrition (i.e., it occurs before the end of the enlisted term of service or ETS), whereas prior-service gains usually enlist for a year or so and, if they separate, do so after having completed their committed term.

Overall, there appears to be an increase in attrition over time among the later cohorts of gains without prior active service. However, the attrition rate of PS gains has remained essentially constant at about 31–32 percent. This difference in pattern could be partially explained if Reserve Components were emphasizing recruiting and retaining PS personnel. On the whole, ODS/S does not appear to have triggered any large effect on attrition behavior.

Differences in attrition among the Reserve Components are seen most clearly when we examine NPS gains, because these reservists are all starting out with no military experience. Figure 7 shows the two-year attrition rate for NPS gains, because there appears to be some instability in the first-year rates. Attrition is highest in the USAR (55 percent for FY92 gains), followed by the ARNG (39 percent), and lowest in the ANG and MCR (20 percent). The two remaining components have attrition rates of 31 (AFR) and 37 percent (NR). A second point to note is that with the exception of the MCR, where attrition actually declined slightly, there has been an increase in attrition—of about 5–10 percentage points—for the FY92–FY93 NPS gain cohorts compared with that of the FY89 cohort. This increase may be partly due to the tightening of training standards or the "creaming" of the gain cohorts in response to the drawdown.

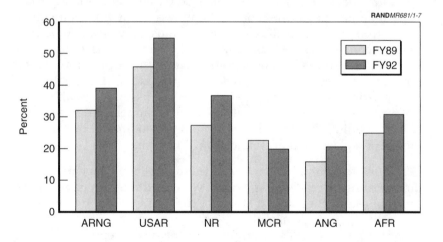

Figure 7—Two-Year Attrition Rates of Nonprior-Service Enlisted Gains by Reserve Component, FY89 and FY92

Table 3 summarizes the recent attrition experience of the Reserve Components for both the inventory as a whole and for gains.

Table 3

Summary of Changes in Attrition Rates, FY89–FY93

Selected Reserve Component	NPS Inventory	PS Inventory	NPS Gains	PS Gains
ARNG	Better	Better	Worse	Stable
USAR	Worse	Better	Worse	Stable
NR	Worse	Worse	Worse	Worse
MCR	Worse	Worse	Better	Better
ANG	Worse	Stable	Worse	Stable
AFR	Stable	Better	Worse	Stable

SKILL QUALIFICATION AND TURBULENCE

Selected Reserve units are frequently not ready for deployment be-cause many members are not skill-qualified in their assigned job. At mobilization, these personnel must be either trained or replaced with qualified personnel before the unit is ready for deployment. Both "fixes" for the qualification have serious drawbacks. Retraining is time-consuming and may strain limited training base resources. Individual training at mobilization disrupts unit preparations for deployment, since individuals involved are not available for preparatory unit exercises. Replacement is disruptive to unit cohe-sion and continuity, since replacement personnel have not trained with the unit. The replacement option is also limited by the avail-ability of replacement personnel from other units.

Skill qualification problems are related to new members joining units and existing or returning members who need retraining. New NPS personnel are sent to a formal service training school and trained in a skill needed in the local unit. PS personnel who are not matched to their active-duty skill are retrained for the new job part-time at the local unit or at a Reserve Component school. Trained personnel fre-quently change jobs in the reserves, so retraining is common. This retraining is generally very time-consuming, since reassigned reservists are seldom retrained full-time.

The skill-qualification rate in the Reserve Components has changed little during the drawdown period. Qualification rates remain low mainly because job and unit turbulence remain high. The frequency of job changes has not abated and job retraining (requalification) is slow.

In 1994, about 30 percent of ARNG and USAR enlisted personnel were unqualified in their assigned skill. The ARNG improvements in prior-service content, better job match of PS personnel, and a smaller training pipeline have reduced the share of unqualified personnel only by 2 or 3 percentage points relative to that of the Cold War era. In the USAR, the rate of unqualified NPS personnel has fallen 15 percentage points since FY86, whereas the rate has been steady for PS personnel. Nonetheless, with 30 percent of personnel unqualified, Army component units will require substantial amounts of retraining or replacement of unqualified members at mobilization.

The skill-qualification rates in the NR have improved substantially in recent years. For the MCR, skill qualification has been somewhat volatile from year to year. The Air components have a somewhat smaller share of unqualified personnel than the other Reserve Components.

Skill qualification remains a serious systemic problem for the reserves. The personnel structure of the reserve fosters widespread job mobility, and requalification of job changers is inherently limited by local reserve facilities and the part-time nature of reserve participation. Reforms are needed to reduce job turbulence both within and across units. When job change is unavoidable, the reserves should focus resources on individual retraining and avoid the pervasive delays that occur under the current system.

CONCLUSIONS AND FUTURE ISSUES

Our analysis suggests that the Reserve Components have improved in a number of respects, although there are clearly remaining areas of concern. The reserves are fielding a senior, very experienced, and high-quality enlisted force, and appear to have been successful in increasing their prior-service content over time (although some components are still short of Title XI goals). This increase is due not so much to the increased affiliation rates of new active losses as to the considerably larger pool of losses created by the drawdown. The components have markedly increased their job-match rates at entry for these new prior-service gains, and first-year attrition rates of these gains have also improved. Inventory attrition has remained remarkably stable over time—clearly, the ODS/S mobilization did not lead to the large outflow feared and predicted by some. Indeed, the attrition rate of PS individuals has remained stable or has declined in some instances. The skill-qualification rate has remained stable during the drawdown period and indicators of job turbulence and unit turbulence show modest improvement. The Selected Reserve Components can be justifiably proud of what they have accomplished in the last five years.

However, the analysis does raise some questions and concerns— some of immediate import and some that will need to be addressed in the future.

Increasing the Supply of PS Personnel

Prior-service personnel remain a critical resource for the Reserve Components because they enhance the experience base and reduce the training requirements. The Reserve Components should investigate further initiatives to increase the affiliation rates of prior-service personnel to the reserves and to improve the utilization of prior-service skills. Several options merit attention.

Joint Active/Reserve Tours. A new Army program formally links a two-year active duty tour with a two-year tour in the Selected Reserves (Buddin and Roan, 1994). A key feature of the program is that Army College Fund monies hinge on successful completion of the active duty obligation *and* subsequent reserve participation. The RC affiliation rate for program participants was 80 percent compared with about 40 percent for nonparticipants. Active/reserve job match was also improved under the program.

Supplemental Educational Benefits. The reserves should consider new programs to provide extra educational benefits to prior-service personnel for affiliating with a reserve unit. Education monies have proven to be a valuable incentive for attracting recruits (Buddin and Roan, 1994) and ongoing research suggests that college-bound personnel are a prime market for the Reserve Components. New educational benefits could be offered selectively when vacancies exist in hard-to-fill skills or high-priority units.

Targeting Incentives. New and reformed programs should place special emphasis on key well-defined reserve needs. Programs are more cost-effective if they are selectively structured to fill vacancies in early-deploying units or critical skills.

Improving Skill-Qualification Rates

Skill qualification remains a serious problem for many Reserve Components. Some of the problem reflects the training pipeline for training nonprior-service personnel when insufficient numbers of prior-service personnel are available to fill reserve vacancies. However, the primary cause of low qualification rates is the high rate of job turbulence in the reserves and subsequent delays in members requalifying in their new skill. We believe that substantive reforms are needed to reduce the rates of job and unit turbulence in the reserves. The reforms would change both the demand- and supply-side incentives to change jobs. On the demand side, the current system encourages units to compete both within and across components for new members. Such competition is frequently counter-productive to the reserves as a whole, since the old unit must recruit and train a new member, and the new unit must generally retrain the transferred member in a new skill. On the supply side, we have seen that members frequently change units, and we hypothesize this is because the promotion prospects are better in the new unit (Buddin and Grissmer, 1994). Ongoing research in this area will help pinpoint the reasons for such turbulence and what reforms might be effective in addressing this issue.

Job retraining and requalification procedures should be reassessed. When members change jobs, the reserves need options to speed re-qualification in the new job. The evidence shows that many members remain unqualified in their duty occupation for many months. The reserves face some inherent problems in retraining personnel locally part-time, but further research is needed to evaluate whether better planning and resource use might substantially reduce retraining time and enhance the skill qualification of reserve units.

To address the issue of skill and unit turbulence, our earlier study (Grissmer et al., 1994a) suggested the establishment of proficiency pay to reward experience and longevity in certain positions where experience is critical to job proficiency. Proficiency pay could be targeted at higher-priority units and higher-priority skills. The amount of pay could vary by skill, grade, and experience. The experience increments could take account of actual active, reserve, and related civilian experience. The additional pay for greater experience could be designed largely to offset the pay advantages of seeking promotion and to give reservists greater incentives to stay in critical positions.

Supply of Nonprior-Service Individuals

A third issue that arises is the future supply of young reservists. It is clear that the near future will see a spate of retirements as the very senior force becomes eligible for retirement, and that the reserve pool of PS individuals—once the active drawdown is completed—will be considerably smaller because of reduced active force sizes. Both of these factors will increase the demand for nonprior-service individuals. However, a number of questions regarding the adequacy of the future supply of these young people remain.

First, the attrition rate for those without prior reserve service has increased over time. As part of the reserve drawdown, this may be deliberate. If not, then it may prove troubling in the future and bears watching. Second, the makeup of the youth population is becoming more ethnically diverse and the propensities of the various ethnic groups to enlist and remain in the reserves is largely unknown. For example, there has been a large influx of Hispanic immigrants over time into the United States; other minority groups, while still small, are also growing as a percentage of the total population. In 1990, the Hispanic population was 22.3 million and this is projected to almost double by the year 2010 (Greenwood, 1994). It is important to understand the propensity of these groups to enlist in the services to more accurately project the supply of nonprior-service enlistments to both the Active and Reserve Components. In addition, if their attrition behavior is different from that of other groups, this will need to be taken into account in manpower requirements projections.

Third, quality may become an important issue. The military is likely to need more highly skilled people as we move to more technologically advanced methods of warfare; at the same time, there is increasing concern regarding the skills and aptitudes of future youth cohorts (this concern may be somewhat exaggerated—see Grissmer et al., 1994b). In any case, the overall question of supply needs to be closely monitored and policy options for increasing reserve supply—such as targeted enlistment and reenlistment bonuses, educational benefits, and shorter enlistment terms aimed at higher-quality recruits—need to be evaluated carefully.

Testing these policies on a limited basis is preferable to full-scale implementation, given the uncertainties of the future environment, force sizes, and force mix. Structured experimentation with many of these policies would help test their effectiveness and determine the best mix of new and old initiatives for addressing the issues raised above.

Aspin, Les, *Report on the Bottom-Up Review,* Department of Defense, October 1993.

Brauner, Marygail K., and Glenn A. Gotz, *Manning Full-Time Positions in Support of the Selected Reserve,* Santa Monica, CA: RAND, R-4034-RA, 1991.

Brauner, Marygail K., Harry J. Thie, and Roger A. Brown, *Assessing the Structure and Mix of Future Active and Reserve Forces: Effectiveness of Total Force Policy During the Persian Gulf Conflict,* Santa Monica, CA: RAND, MR-132-OSD, 1992.

Buddin, Richard J., and David W. Grissmer, *Skill Qualification and Turbulence in the Army National Guard and Army Reserve,* Santa Monica, CA: RAND, MR-289-RA, 1994.

Buddin, Richard J., and Stephen J. Kirin, *Army Reserve Component Accessions from Personnel Completing Their First Active-Duty Enlistment,* Santa Monica, CA: RAND, MR-258-A, 1994.

Buddin, Richard J., and Carole E. Roan, *Assessment of Combined Active/Reserve Recruiting Programs,* Santa Monica, CA: RAND, MR-504-A, 1994.

Department of Defense, *Reserve Component Program, Fiscal Year 1993: Report of the Reserve Forces Policy Board,* January 1994.

Greenwood, Michael J., "Immigrants and the U.S. Military: History and Prospects," in Mark J. Eitelberg and Stephen L. Mehay (eds.),

Marching Toward the 21st Century: Military Manpower and Recruiting, Westport, CT: Greenwood Press, 1994.

Grissmer, David W., and Sheila Nataraj Kirby, "A Total Force Perspective on Recruiting and Manning in the Years Ahead," in Mark J. Eitelberg and Stephen L. Mehay (eds.), *Marching Toward the 21st Century: Military Manpower and Recruiting,* Westport, CT: Greenwood Press, 1994.

Grissmer, David W., and Glenda Nogami, *Retention Patterns for Army National Guard Units Attending the National Training Center (NTC),* Alexandria, VA: U.S. Army Research Institute, 1988.

Grissmer, David W., Richard J. Buddin, and Sheila Nataraj Kirby, *Improving Reserve Compensation: A Review of Current Compensation and Related Personnel and Training-Readiness Issues,* Santa Monica, CA: RAND, R-3707-FMP/RA, 1989.

Grissmer, David W., Sheila Nataraj Kirby, and Man-bing Sze, *Factors Affecting Reenlistment of Reservists: Spouse and Employer Attitudes and Perceived Unit Environment,* Santa Monica, CA: RAND, R-4011-RA, 1992.

Grissmer, David W., Sheila Nataraj Kirby, Richard Buddin, Jennifer H. Kawata, Jerry M. Sollinger, and Stephanie Williamson, *Prior Service Personnel: A Potential Constraint on Increasing Reliance on Reserve Forces,* Santa Monica, CA: RAND, MR-362-OSD, 1994a.

Grissmer, David W., Sheila Nataraj Kirby, Mark Berends, and Stephanie Williamson, *Student Achievement and the Changing American Family,* Santa Monica, CA: RAND, MR-488-LE, 1994b.

Kirby, Sheila N., and David W. Grissmer, *Reassessing Enlisted Reserve Attrition: A Total Force Perspective,* Santa Monica, CA: RAND, N-3521-RA, 1993.

Marquis, M. Susan, and Sheila Nataraj Kirby, *Reserve Accessions Among Individuals with Prior Military Service: Supply and Skill Match,* Santa Monica, CA: RAND, R-3892-RA 1989.

U.S. House of Representatives, *National Defense Authorization Act of Fiscal Year 1993,* House Report 102-966.